Living on Earth

CONCEPT SCIENCE

Written by Colin Walker • Illustrated by Caroline Campbell

People live on many different parts
of the earth's surface.

Some people live in houses
built on the ice.

Some people live in tents
on the sandy surface of the desert.

A long time ago, people used to live in caves.

Homes give us shelter.
Homes may be made of . . .

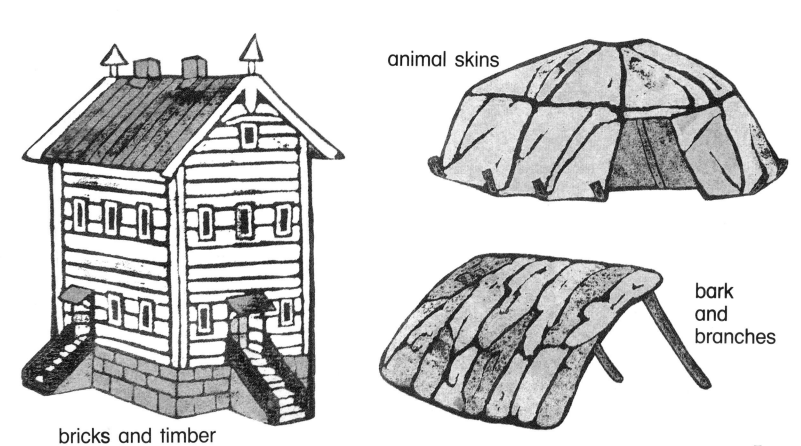

animal skins

bark
and
branches

bricks and timber

Wherever people live,
they always need a home
that is close to food and water.

6

Water is important to people
all over the world.

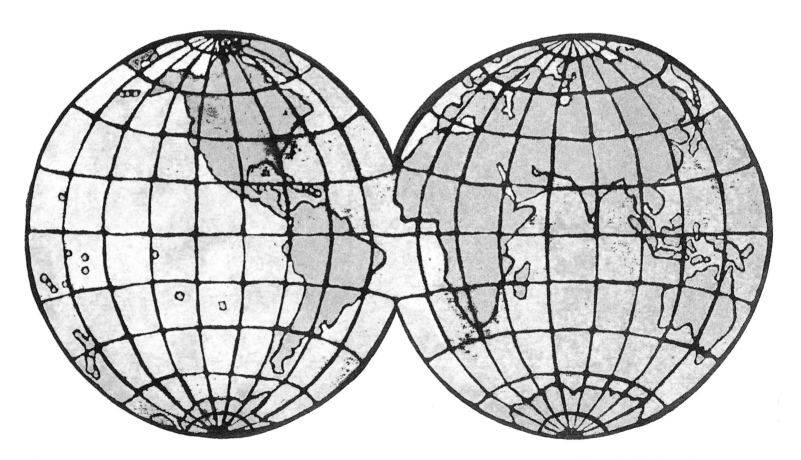

Most people live near fresh water
because they need water to drink.
They also need water for their animals
and crops.

People use water to carry their goods
from place to place.

junk

container ship

canoe

barge

raft

11

If there is no water nearby,
people build roads and railways
across the surface of the earth.
Then they can carry goods
from place to place.

Roads and railways are even built
under mountains and on bridges.

Wherever people live on earth,
they need food, water, and shelter.

QUIZ

Ask your friend these questions. . .

Where may an  be built?

Some people live in tents in the

What did people use to live in
a long, long time ago?

Try these activities:

1. Homes give us shelter. Close your eyes and think about your home. Write a paragraph about your home and draw a picture of it. Explain what you like best about your home and how your home makes your life more comfortable.

2. With a friend, make a mobile that shows what you need to live on Earth. Find or draw pictures that show the food, water, and shelter you use every day. Tape your pictures to string and attach them to a coat hanger to make a mobile. Share your mobile with the class.